QuickGUIDES

everything you need to know...fast

HANDLING THE MEDIA
Strategies for Success

by Jo Pearson
reviewed by Cherry Bushell

Across the world the organizations and institutions that fundraise to finance their work are referred to in many different ways. They are charities, non-profits or not-for-profit organizations, non-governmental organizations (NGOs), voluntary organizations, academic institutions, agencies, etc. For ease of reading, we have used the term Nonprofit Organization, Organization or NPO as an umbrella term throughout the *Quick*Guide series. We have also used the spellings and punctuation used by the author.

Published by
Wiremill Publishing Ltd.
Edenbridge, Kent TN8 5PS, UK
info@wiremillpublishing.com
www.wiremillpublishing.com
www.quickguidesonline.com

British Library Cataloguing in Publication Data
A catalogue record for this book is available from the British Library.

ISBN Number 1-905053-22-3

Printed by Rhythm Consolidated Berhad, Malaysia
Cover Design by Jennie de Lima and Edward Way
Design by Colin Woodman Design

Contents

Handling the Media

Strategies for Success

Introduction

The media can be a great help to nonprofit organisations (NPOs). They provide a vehicle by which great numbers of people can find out about your organisation and its work. They can also cause concern, particularly if something goes wrong and no one is prepared to handle the public consequences.

This *Quick*Guide will provide you with a sound working knowledge of what journalists are looking for when they come to you for a story, how best to prepare for media attention, and how you can successfully manage a media encounter. By understanding what makes the media tick, you will be better placed to use them to your advantage and get your message across. When you have a positive story, you will be able to deliver it to the benefit of your organisation; when your organisation is the subject of a story less complimentary or downright derogatory, you will be able to deal with it in the best way possible.

No matter whether it's the evening prime-time news on television, the morning programme on radio or the inside front page of the national newspaper, there is the added bonus of exposure – for free! Make the most of it!

The media can provide a superb opportunity to project a good image of your organisation to the broadest constituency possible. Working with, rather than against, the media will help ensure that you are pleased with the final result.

Be Prepared

Be prepared for dealing with the media. You must be prepared in terms of your material and information, your appearance and presentation. This applies right across the board, from the way you handle your first contact with a print journalist, programme producer or researcher right through to the interview.

Reviewer's Comment

Have some sort of "crisis PR" plan for media emergencies of any type. This is more about your process for handling a crisis than trying to identify every issue that might arise, which could be a completely unexpected problem or event.

Start with the initial contact. If you are contacting the media for an opportunity to talk about something your organisation is doing, you will be in control of the time and method of communication. If the media are contacting you for a response to something that has occurred or for a story, the contact will be at their time of choosing. Whenever you receive a call from the media, you or your staff should immediately note the caller's name and company and exactly what he or she is seeking.

It may be a request for an interview later in the day, or it may be a radio station wanting to put you on-air immediately. If you are skilled at dealing with the media, are on top of the situation that has led to the call, and have already prepared your most important, or *key messages*, you might decide to go ahead with the interview there and then.

If you are not the person who is authorised and best equipped to deal with the media, you should say so, offer to find the appropriate person, and say you will be back in touch within a deadline-friendly time frame.

Continues on next page

Reviewer's Comment
Organisations should choose the best person to perform the role of spokesperson, rather than the most senior or the most expert. You can always brief a less knowledgeable but "media friendly" person, but you can't do much to improve, say, a director with a less than winning personality or an expert who can't talk in layman's terms.

Don't be pressured. You have every right to put some vital preparation time between this first contact and an interview.

You may decide that an alternative strategy to the one-on-one interview is advisable, such as issuing a media release, conducting a media conference or making a media statement.

Key Messages and Your Approach

Key Messages

In any interview or preparation for dealing with the media, the questions asked by the reporter are not the most important concern. Your identification of key messages and your ability to get them across are what matter most of all. Techniques to deliver the key messages are discussed later in this *Quick*Guide. Key messages should be written down and refined for succinctness, clarity, simplicity, and impact.

As part of this preparation, it is vital to list the areas where you might be vulnerable to negative lines of questioning and seriously consider your *position* on these issues. You should also be able to talk about positive facts and areas of success.

Choose powerful and interesting language, keep ideas short and simple, and test whether your message effectively cuts off a negative line of questioning and gets across positive issues successfully.

Your Approach

Your mental approach to any dealings with the media is crucial. The journalist can be a great ally and a powerful promotional vehicle for your organisation. Those who proactively seek the media's attention generally do so with a positive feeling toward them. But if the media contact you, your reaction may be defensive or negative.

You need to take on a positive frame of mind no matter who contacts whom. If the media come to you, they are there for information, unless you are dealing with a crisis. You are the expert. You have the information they need. Even when the news is bad, you can still acquit yourself well and avoid a great deal of damage to your organisation by approaching the media questions positively.

Any dealing with the media is a chance to project a favourable image. Contributors, potential benefactors, alumni, employees, volunteers, clients, regulators, and other stakeholders of your organisation all watch television, listen to the radio and read newspapers.

Perceptions and Background Briefings

Perceptions

Although the media have an important role in disseminating information, journalists are considered by many to be a law unto themselves. Yet most journalists are decent, hard-working individuals who value their craft and respect its power.

That craft is providing information. Every day, newspapers, radio stations and TV channels have more space and time to fill.

As long as you have a story to tell or questions to answer, your organisation is interesting to the media. You can provide them with material, which they require in order to fill programmes, and they can provide an outlet for you. However, once you are no longer newsworthy, you simply do not matter anymore. Although the subject might be dear to your heart, it is *just another story* to the media. So use the opportunities presented to you because they often disappear almost immediately.

Background Briefings

Sometimes you will want to provide information to the media without it being attributed either to you personally or to the organisation. This may be particularly true when dealing with a sensitive issue which would best be handled without the organisation appearing to be involved. Organisations dealing with contentious public issues, for example, may find this method of communicating appropriate.

On these occasions, you can brief journalists without appearing in an interview or being quoted directly. This is a legitimate method of releasing information to the media.

Generally, reporters will respect your confidence and attribute the information to *"reliable sources"* or say something as vague as *"it is understood."* It is advisable that the background briefing strategy be limited to reputable journalists and media organisations with which you have an ongoing relationship.

Television

Television news and current affairs are looking for a mix of interesting vision, strong human interest, and perhaps some conflicting views to provide a dramatic element. Whatever the duration of the report, the object is to compress a sometimes complicated story into a short amount of time and dress it up visually with a number of complimentary and contrary views.

For a news report, there will be at least one reporter's *piece-to-camera,* a couple of short, linking *voice-overs* and two or three short interview *sound bites.*

Television provides the opportunity to tell your story visually. It can also be the trickiest medium for the inexperienced.

Your demeanour and the impression you make on the journalist will influence the way you are treated in the final product. Handle yourself well, be calm and courteous, and you will probably get a fair story.

Television current-affairs programming is a particularly hungry animal, with much on-air time available for each story. If your organisation is being asked to appear on television rather than seeking to be there, it may be because there has been a problem with your organisation or another and you are being asked to take part as a knowledgeable party.

You need to understand that confrontation is frequently an essential element of television. If there is no direct confrontation, it may be manufactured in the editing process. This upsets many people who believe they are being quoted out of context. Unfortunately, it is an accepted part of the editing process and is something that one must learn to live with.

Radio

Radio has an even more insatiable need than television to find stories and fill programming time. *Talk* stations not only must have programmes but also must provide information to their news services. They are always looking for a new angle, a fresh lead or a new sound bite. If your organisation is involved in a contentious situation, you can expect to be deluged with calls from very persistent journalists. If you have information you want to tell people about, radio can provide an excellent outlet for information – whether it is an upcoming fundraising event, new treatment developed by your researchers, or top academic marks obtained by your students.

But it is the story that comes to you – something that your organisation is involved in, good or bad, or something about which your organisation is asked to comment – which causes the most concern, but it need not if you understand how to handle yourself.

Individuals may find themselves awakened in the early morning by radio news reporters. The journalists will want to conduct a phone interview then and there so they have a sound bite for their prime-time morning news services.

Reporters will contact the representative of the organisation who has the connection with the media. Telephone calls can come anytime during the day!

If you are prepared for such an interview, fine. If not, it is imperative that you buy some time. Firmly and politely tell the callers that you cannot discuss the matter at that moment, but you will be back in touch with them shortly. Take down their details. Ask what the story is about, who else might be involved and what they said.

Assume that everything you say is being recorded. Remain friendly and professional but in control. Don't be led into commenting by the persistence of the reporters.

It is vitally important that you have time to wake up; gather information; perhaps consult with others; and determine your strategy, position statements and key messages. Make sure that you or a representative gets back to the journalists to let them know what you can do for them – ideally, in time for the major morning bulletins.

There may also be times when you will be asked to go into the radio studio.

It is important to ask if anyone else will be on the programme with you so that you are not unsettled by a *surprise* guest waiting on another line. Knowing who else may be involved in the story will give you a better idea of the angle the interviewer is taking and help you decide whether you want to be involved in the likely debate.

Before agreeing to an interview with a *talk-back* host (a programme where the public can call in and ask questions of the guest), you also need to stipulate whether you are happy to take listeners' calls. If your interview is contentious, people will call the station and want their say. A talk-back situation can be unpredictable and difficult to handle. It is not advisable for the inexperienced.

Newspapers

Just as television and radio need stories, so do the print media, providing yet another avenue for you to reach the public with the information you are trying to disseminate.

A one-page press release on the issue you want covered is a good way to start communication between you and the journalist. The journalist can then follow up if interested in the information.

Alternatively, the journalist will contact you if there is a story, good or bad.

Newspaper interviews will be conducted by telephone or in person. Contrary to popular belief, they require just as much, if not more, preparation than radio or television interviews. The most frequent complaint about dealing with the media is that print journalists misquote or quote out of context in their articles.

Interview subjects often contribute to this problem by not preparing their information suitably. Print media may seem to have more time and space for more detailed coverage, but in reality, print journalists work under similar constraints of time and space.

Prepare your positioning statement and three or four key messages, just as you would for the electronic media.

Check what articles that particular journalist has written recently – you might be able to identify which issues he or she tends to focus on, and you will have an insight into the readership's level of comprehension.

A page of concisely written details about your organisation may be useful to the reporter. If feasible, prepare a one-page media release on the relevant issue and give it to the journalist as a form of background information.

Do not be afraid to spell the names of people aloud – the journalist may still get them wrong, but perhaps with fewer errors.

Your most important audience in a print interview is the person sitting opposite you. Your job is not just to answer his or her questions but also to communicate your key messages and to convince that journalist of your professionalism, credibility and honesty.

Your vocal tone, emphasis, facial expressions, and body language are all part of making sure you are at your convincing best. Your greeting, hospitality, eye contact, tone and warmth will also make an indelible impression upon the person who *wields the pen.*

Interview Techniques

Nothing can be as daunting as facing an interviewer in front of a camera, in a radio station with headphones on, or with a tape recorder writing furiously as you speak.

No matter whether you have initiated the interview as part of a publicity campaign or the media have come to you, you will want to make a good impression. The following information and tips will help you deal effectively and confidently with an interviewer from any of the three types of media.

Reviewer's Comment
Role-playing media interviews with your colleagues will help you prepare for the real thing. It may also identify who is best suited to be spokesperson, if you are unsure whom to select.

No Comment

There are probably no two words uttered to the media that are more damaging. They imply guilt or that you have something to hide. You might not want to comment for any number of reasons, but you should say something – even if it is to articulate a willingness to help, to ask details of what the journalist needs and in what time frame.

If you are not in a position to make a comment or be interviewed, say so, but provide a good reason. It might be that you are not the most appropriate person or you have not had time to be fully briefed. It might be a matter that is under investigation or in legal hands.

Off the Record

There is no such thing as "off the record" when you are dealing with the media. Even if you know the journalist and believe he or she can be trusted, you should not say things *off the record* unless you intend for them to be published.

On returning to the office, the journalist might mention your comments to the producer or news editor. If what you said is newsworthy, maybe even sensational, the journalist will be asked to include it in the story.

The remarks might not be attributed directly to you, but when they appear as an unnamed source, your colleagues may identify the comments as coming from you.

Interview Techniques

Interviews Are "Live"

You should assume that microphones, cameras and journalists are always switched on. This assumption should apply to every aspect of your dealings with the media, from the initial contact until you bid them goodbye.

For example, radio stations may already be recording when they call you. They regularly deal with experienced interviewees who know that they are being recorded, and the interviewer may not know the level of your experience or inexperience.

Television interviews can also be a trap for the unwary. You might be in the studio waiting for the interview to formally begin. To help you settle your nerves, you might chat with the interviewer.

The journalist could quite legitimately use what you said while chatting once the interview starts. Worse still, your microphone may already have been broadcasting your comments to other studios around the country!

If the videotape is rolling, unknown to you, your aside could end up in the edited report, or the interviewer might take your light-hearted comment and pose it to you as a question.

You should also be on your guard at the end of an interview, whether it is in a studio or in your office. By this stage, people are usually relieved that the interview is over and let their guard down. Yet, the microphones are often left on; even though the interview seems to be finished, anything you say or do is being recorded and could be used.

Be Honest

If you try to hoodwink the media, you stand a very good chance of being discovered. Television, in particular, is a great lie detector.

You might be in a situation where you do not want to lie but also do not want to divulge certain information. You may genuinely wish to protect a colleague or an employee from unwarranted claims, or you may not wish to publicly discuss certain information at that particular time.

Simply be honest. Tell the interviewer politely but firmly that you are not in a position to comment on that matter, and give the reasons why without going into great detail. At the same time, indicate your willingness to discuss other matters and do so fully and frankly.

Continues on next page

Reviewer's Comment
I can't stress enough the importance of being honest and accurate. This not only results in a good interview but also ensures a good relationship with the interviewer.

Be Accurate

Make sure you have done your research. Canvass all of the relevant issues with your colleagues and review them yourself. If you are dealing with figures and statistics, get them right, keep them simple and try to make them as interesting as possible.

If you have to use figures, try to contextualise with simple examples. If you are being criticised for the cost of administering a fundraising campaign, for instance, relate the cost to the total benefit that the effort is delivering. You could further deflect the damage by referring to the cost minimisation strategies that you have in place.

If you need notes to remind you of exact figures, put them to one side when you do your television interview. Most reporters will ask you to put down any papers before the interview starts. There's nothing more distracting to the viewer than a person who keeps referring to notes.

Answering Questions

Do not be surprised if at times the questions seem inept or naive.

The reporter may genuinely not understand something that is a simple fact or everyday occurrence to you. Then again, he or she may understand very well, yet needs to ask the question on behalf of an audience or readership that probably does not.

The youth of some reporters and their apparent lack of knowledge about certain matters may surprise you.

Do not show your annoyance or impatience with any of this. It is the viewer who will be the ultimate recipient of your *attitude.* Answer the questions to the best of your ability and in a way that does not reflect on your view of the interviewer.

If the journalist uses exaggerated language or incorrect information in a question, your responsibility is to set the record straight. Do not repeat the language that the journalist uses because this can give it some credibility – even in denial. Phrases like *"That is not how I would describe the situation"* or *"That's not the case"* are preferable to repeating negative, overly colourful or incorrect material.

There may be times when you genuinely lose your way or need to clear your throat. If that happens, say so, and politely ask for the question again.

If you are confronted with a question that concerns you greatly, you can politely decline to answer because, for example, it means you would have to speak on behalf of others, discuss matters that are the subject of an investigation or inquiry, or comment on material you have not read.

Offering to brief the reporter is always worthwhile, and usually this can be done in a separate room while the crew is setting up. Always offer concise *background* information about your organisation or an information sheet pertaining to the subject that is about to be discussed.

It's also a good idea to prepare an up-to-date media release. Often the journalist will arrive at your office with nothing more than a copy of a newspaper article, which may contain inaccurate or outdated information. If you provide an accurate update, there is every chance the information will be used. It also gives you a chance to once again stress the three or four key issues or the message you have come to deliver.

Surprises

You should always be on guard for any agenda the journalist may bring to an interview. Without warning, a new issue could be introduced into the discussion. You are well within your rights to point out that you are there to be interviewed on a specific subject. If the interviewer persists, suggest that you would be more than happy to deal with those questions at a later date, when you have had time to obtain all the relevant information.

It is important that you ask what the *line of questioning* is going to be. Reporters are unlikely to give you the exact questions they are going to ask, or they might give you just the "easy" ones.

When you arrive for a studio interview, you might be in for a shock if you haven't previously asked, *"Who else will*

Continues on next page

be involved in the story?" There may be another guest – perhaps a detractor waiting to do battle. Some programmes will introduce the guest once the interview has started, which can leave you in an awkward, no-win situation.

If you have agreed to a studio interview, and it is some hours away, it is essential that you ask again, closer to the interview, whether anyone else is involved in the story and what issues are to be discussed. Another party may have become involved or the story may have taken a new turn since you last spoke to the reporter or producer.

IN THE HOT SEAT

Your posture is an important part of your presentation in a television interview. Find a comfortable upright position. You can move a little, using your hands and facial expressions as you would in a normal conversation. Try not to do anything in an exaggerated or repetitive way, and make sure you don't hit the microphone with your hand gestures. DON'T TAP!

Try to forget the camera and the crew; keep your eyes on the interviewer.

Some reporters do their interviews without referring to notes, while others look down from time to time. Ignore them when they do and, although it may feel a little strange, do not move your eyes – even if you are looking at the top of the reporter's head.

THE "SIX C'S"

CONCISE, CALM, COURTEOUS, CAUTIOUS, CONVERSATIONAL, and in CONTROL

The "six c's" are fundamental in your dealings with the media.

Being *concise* is essential. Normally you will get a better deal from a journalist, whether from print or electronic media, if you have prepared your material to be succinct, clear and simple.

Reporters hate nothing more than having to wade through convoluted, rambling statements. They want simple answers, delivered without jargon. Avoid the use of acronyms and highly technical terms. Use plain English (if you're speaking English!).

Calm and *courteous* go hand in hand. You must stay calm no matter what the provocation. There might be extreme situations where you feel fully justified in losing your temper, but do not.

However, you must be prepared for confrontation if your contact with the media is the result of a contentious story. It is part of a simple media formula. Get two parties screaming at each other and you have a *hot* story.

Although you must remain calm, you need to be forceful in getting your point across if the interviewer or your opponent, if you have one, is being deliberately provocative or misleading.

If statements or claims are totally outrageous, say so, and suggest to the interviewer that you are quite happy to continue to discuss relevant matters.

Questions that contain misinformation or vague generalisations must be challenged. For instance, if the interviewer says, *"Many people are saying"* or *"It's widely understood,"* the inference is that the interviewer has a wealth of research and information which forms the basis of the question.

Reviewer's Comment
Feel free to ask the interviewer for specifics about those people who are saying something or who widely understand. Don't do it in an adversarial manner.

Often the opposite is the case and the questions are based on the flimsiest of evidence. The interviewer is simply *fishing for a response*, hoping that you will take the bait.

Do not answer any hypothetical questions. Do not be bullied. Ask politely for proof of the assumption in the question.

Exercise *caution* in your answers and avoid the trap of filling the interviewer's pauses with admissions or extra information that has not been asked for. Limit your answers only to what needs to be said, focussing on your key positive phrases. Don't bring up past problem areas that the interviewer hasn't mentioned.

Where possible, be more *conversational* than formal in your tone. A good interview sounds like a good

Continues on next page

conversation, even if you feel that the reporter is being hostile or provocative.

Unlike a conversation, you should look for opportunities to repeat your positioning statements and key messages. It is advisable to make your important points more than once.

When you sit down to do a television interview, you must try to shut out much of what is going on around you. You are not likely to forget that you are on television and you must be aware there is a wider audience, but your most important task is to communicate with the person sitting in front of you. Look the interviewer in the eye – he or she is your audience.

Remember, also, that the interviewer's questions are often left out of the final report – especially in news stories. The questions are simply a device to elicit a suitable sound bite.

LOCATIONS

If the interview is to be conducted on your premises, arrange a suitable location beforehand. Use your office, if appropriate, because it is your territory and you will feel more at ease.

Camera crews do not like plain white walls or windows that allow the sun to stream in. They like to control the lighting. There will need to be sufficient space for the crew to set up and two chairs (preferably the same height, to keep the eye line similar, and the type that doesn't swivel, to keep you in one place). The crew will probably rearrange your office, but don't worry because they are usually very careful.

Office noise, such as loud conversations, public announcement systems and air-conditioners, can cause problems for a television or radio crew. It is important that loud electronic equipment is, if possible, turned off for the duration of the interview and staff members are asked not to interrupt the proceedings.

If it is not an emergency situation, arrange parking and offer light refreshments to the reporter and camera crew. Often they are in need of a tea or coffee break. Apart from being good manners, it does have a psychological effect. It may help influence the way the final product is packaged.

Interview Techniques

Grooming and Dress

How you look and present yourself is important for a television interview. You should dress as formally as your situation and climate dictate.

A white shirt, without a jacket, can be a problem. White tends to confuse the electronics of the camera and it can be too bright on a sunny day. Both men and women should also avoid wearing fabrics with heavy checks and stripes. These tend to *strobe,* or jump about on the screen. Strobing is very distracting for the viewer and may detract from the message you are trying to get across.

If you normally wear a suit, then do so. If you wear a tie, make sure the tie knot is securely in place and perfectly centred before you start the interview.

Women should avoid frills, flounces, stripes and bold prints because these will dominate the screen. Ensure your hair is tidy and won't fall over your eyes during the interview.

You need to be careful with the amount and style of jewellery so that it is not too distracting or noisy if you *talk with your hands.*

Tape Recorders

As a matter of course, you should tape any interview you do with the media. Just before the interview starts, simply produce a small tape recorder and, without fanfare or comment, place it on your desk. This serves a number of purposes. It immediately puts the journalist on notice that you expect the final report to accurately reflect the interview that is about to begin, and it also provides an accurate record of the interview which you can use later if you feel you have been unfairly treated. In addition, it's a useful tool for reviewing and revising your performance.

Be Yourself

Another cardinal rule when dealing with the media, especially television and radio, is to *be yourself.* Often people will assume another persona once the camera starts rolling. They believe they have to be different, pompous or larger-than-life, and in the process, their credibility and their effectiveness suffer.

Not everyone is an extrovert or a great communicator, but your skills can be improved with preparation and practice. Remember, if you are asked to do an

Continues on next page

interview, it is because you are regarded by your organisation, or by the media, as an expert in your field.

The public wants to be informed and reassured by you. At the same time, people want to feel that they are being spoken to by someone who is approachable and reflects the same concerns they have. They want to know that you are responsible, caring, in control – but above all, human.

A natural smile, when appropriate, makes an enormous impression on those watching your face intently. To avoid a forced expression, try to think of *smiling with your eyes.* The rest of your face will naturally follow.

Don't hesitate to use the words "I" and "me" in your answers. The public has tired of hearing standard corporate responses and the obvious "*organisational line.*" They will warm to you and your message knowing that you share their concerns and take personal responsibility seriously.

Above all, the public and your stakeholders are reassured by the fact that the *public face* of your organisation is caring and compassionate, and that you have the courage to speak publicly – especially when something has gone wrong.

If you stick to the basics by being well prepared and by remaining courteous, calm and in control – even when things get really tough – you will not only survive your media encounters but will also acquit yourself and those you represent.

Final Thoughts

You Never Know When ...

After reading this *Quick*Guide, you should have a better understanding of the media and media management techniques. Make sure that you are not the only individual within your organisation equipped with this valuable knowledge. You will need others within your team to assist you when the media call – often at a moment's notice.

If the media called today, and you had just an hour or two to react, would you have the resources to make the most of this opportunity to get your message across? Do you have someone within your organisation to help you develop and practice your *positioning statements* and *key messages* and write a media release? Do you have written *background information* about your organisation to hand or email to journalists? Do others within your organisation know how to handle media enquiries? At the very least, your telephone answering procedures should ensure that you know who has called, where they are from, what the enquiry is about, and what their deadline is.

Exposure is a valuable opportunity if you are facing negative public scrutiny; if the media have sought your assistance in covering a story on social, health or educational issues; or if you have sought media attention as part of a public relations or marketing campaign. When the news is positive, publicity through the various media outlets is a lifeline. When the news is negative, your handling of the media will speak volumes about the professionalism, accountability and values of your organisation.

Although the media may sometimes seem interested in talking to organisations only when the news is bad, they can be powerful allies in getting your message across to more people than you could ever hope to reach with your own resources. That is why it is so important that you and your organisation are not only *media-wise* but also *media-ready* at all times.

Author

Jo Pearson

Jo Pearson has more than 20 years' experience as a news reporter, media trainer and writer. Born and raised in the UK, Jo presented news as a journalist, producer and reporter for Australian and American news services from the age of 17. In 1977, she became a senior prime-time television newsreader, and one of Australia's youngest and best-known on-air news personalities.

As founder and director of the Melbourne-based media consultancy Media Strategies, Jo delivers quality training programmes and multimedia training material to her clients.

Jo's journalistic training began with a cadetship at a metropolitan daily newspaper and formal journalism studies at the University of Queensland, in Brisbane, Australia. After graduating, she worked as a newspaper reporter and features writer, radio news presenter and live radio broadcaster, as well as a senior television news reporter and presenter.

Jo was part of the top-rated reporting team at TV station KCRA 3 Sacramento in California in 1980. Two years later, she returned to Australia to co-host Melbourne's top-rated Eyewitness News Service. In 1987, she gained national exposure as a presenter on a range of programmes for the Television Nine Network.

Since 1990, Jo has developed and delivered tailored media training and advice to a range of NPOs, corporate and government clients, organisations, athletes and educators. During this time, she has also become one of Australia's most highly regarded media trainers and corporate speakers.

Jo has extensive experience as a public speaker, master of ceremonies and facilitator. She has written and produced training, promotional and informational films and videos for Australian businesses.

Cherry Bushell, Reviewer

Cherry Bushell has extensive experience in all aspects of charity and nonprofit work, both on the administration side and the fundraising side. She worked with one of the UK's largest charities, Macmillan Cancer Relief, where she managed a variety of fundraising mechanisms with national, small and medium-sized companies, as well as trusts, foundations and individual donors. She directed promotional and special events, and ran a community programme which involved coordinating committee networks, retail outlets, youth and school groups, and local volunteer associations. In her work with smaller charities, Cherry raised funds by means of corporate partnerships, social and sporting events, trusts, major donors, auctions and celebrity endorsements. In particular, she was responsible for liaising with celebrities, the royal patron and other high-profile supporters. Interacting with staff, volunteers and the general community has been an ongoing part of Cherry's career.

Cherry has a BA (Hons) degree in Modern History, Economic History and Politics.